Cook's
NOTES

Canadian representatives: General Publishing Co., Ltd.,
30 Lesmill Road, Don Mills, Ontario M3B 2T6.

9 8 7 6 5 4 3 2 1
Digit on the right indicates the number of this printing.

ISBN 1–56138–580–8

Cover design by Toby Schmidt
Cover and interior illustrations by Valerie Coursen
Interior design by Susan E. Van Horn
Edited by William King
Typography by Justin T. Scott
Printed in the United States

This book may be ordered by mail from the publisher.
Please add $1.00 for postage and handling.
But try your bookstore first!

Running Press Book Publishers
125 South Twenty-second Street
Philadelphia, Pennsylvania 19103–4399

Cook's

N O T E S

RUNNING PRESS
PHILADELPHIA · LONDON

I cook like a bird sings.

Michael Guerard
20th-century French chef

Good cooking is not only friend, wife and lover, but playmate, hobby, craft, encounter group and psychotherapist.

WILLIAM RICE (B. 1912)
AMERICAN RAILROAD OFFICIAL

. . . I was deeply infatuated with
the food processor from the first.
I loved the way it bossed food
around. . . .

Frieda Garmaise (b. 1928)
American writer

The only way to learn to cook is to cook.

Alice B. Toklas (1877–1967)
American writer

Cookery means the knowledge of Medea and of Circe. . . . It means the knowledge of all herbs and fruits . . . and all that is healing and sweet in the fields and groves. . . .

JOHN RUSKIN (1819–1900)
ENGLISH WRITER

*C*ookery is become an art, a noble
science; cooks are gentlemen.

Robert Burton (1577–1640)
English cleric and writer

The cook was a good cook, as cooks go;

and as good cooks go, she went.

Saki [H.H. Munro] (1870–1916)
Scottish writer

I am loath to trust that cook who maintains she constantly practices
her craft and gaineth never a pound.

DINAH SHORE (1920–1994)
AMERICAN SINGER AND ENTERTAINER

The cook holds the balance of power, and ofttimes sways destinies: the overthrow of Grease, the downfall of China, the dividing of Turkey—what cook has not accomplished all of these in one short lifetime?

Fables of a Rolling-Pin

. . . organization is just as important in
the kitchen as in any business office. . . .

DIONE LUCAS (1909–1971)
ENGLISH-AMERICAN CHEF

If you have great ingredients to work with, it makes you happy all day long.

Thomas Catherall
20th-century English-born American chef

'Tis an ill cook that cannot lick his own fingers.

William Shakespeare (1564–1616)
English dramatist and poet

*I*f you are surprised at the number of our maladies,

count our cooks.

LUCIUS ANNAEUS SENECA (4 B.C.–65 A.D.)
ROMAN PHILOSOPHER, WRITER, AND POLITICIAN

Classic cuisine is to nouvelle cuisine what classical ballet is to neoclassical ballet. In cooking as in the dance, one cannot do the second one well without being thoroughly familiar with the first.

Madeleine Kamman (b. 1918)
French chef

. . . loving to cook is not necessarily loving to cook *well*.

John Thorne (b. 1943)
American writer

*C*uisine is when things taste like themselves.

Curnonsky [Maurice Saillant] (1872–1956)
French chef and journalist

When you don't like to cook, you're
undoubtedly talented and energetic
in other ways. . . .

PEG BRACKEN (B. 1920)
AMERICAN WRITER

*P*ersonal liberation for me was also

incidentally culinary liberation. . . .

Norman Rush (b. 1933)
American writer

Every man should eat and drink and enjoy the fruit of all his labor.

Ecclesiastes 5:18

The chief pleasure [in eating] does not consist in costly seasoning,
or exquisite flavor, but in yourself.

HORACE (65–8 B.C.)
ROMAN POET

Certainly, food is not the only way to show love, but it is one of the pleasantest and simplest.

Barbara Kafka (b. 1933)
American writer

No one should be deprived of the pleasure and quality of life that
beautifully prepared food and a little wine can bring. . . .

JULIA CHILD (B. 1912)
AMERICAN WRITER AND CHEF

*L*et the dishes be few in number, but exquisitely chosen.

Anthelme Brillat-Savarin (1775–1826)
French politician and writer

Cooking is a way of giving and making yourself desirable.

Michel Bourdin
20th-century French chef

Food and beauty are human nature.

CONFUCIUS (C. 551–479 B.C.)
CHINESE PHILOSOPHER

If beautifully presented, anything tastes better!

Elizabeth Taylor (b. 1932)
British-born American actress

"I read somewhere that cooking is one of the three human activities that occupy the exact middle ground between nature and art."

"What are the others?"

"Gardening. . . . And sex."

Rosie Thomas (b. 1947)
English writer

$\mathcal{L}$et your plate be your canvas.

ROSIE DALEY
20TH-CENTURY AMERICAN CHEF

Cooking food, laughing and story telling—that's what we're made of and that's what we enjoy the most.

Ernest Matthew Mickler (1940–1988)
American writer

There is little difference between dining and eating. Dining is an art. When you eat to please the palate, as well as to satiate the appetite, that, my friend, is dining.

Martin Yan (b. 1951)
Chinese chef

๑๑

. . . but food eaten quickly isn't food.

Aleksandr Solzhenitsyn (b. 1918)
Russian writer

*S*ince cooking is an art, the French approach eating with the same attitude as they would a painting or a concert: it should principally satisfy the sense involved.

FERNANDE GARVIN
20TH-CENTURY FRENCH CHEF

There is something that is associated with a homemade dessert that evokes among all of us a sense of comfort and well-being—it is a gift of love.

Nancy Silverton
20th-century American chef

Modest intimacy descended upon the kitchen. It came, somehow, from the cooking. Fixing supper for a stranger, with him chopping turnips . . . beside you, removed some of the strangeness.

Robert James Waller (b. 1939)
American writer

For those who love it, cooking is at once
child's play and adult joy. And cooking
done with care is an act of love.

CRAIG CLAIBORNE (B. 1920)
AMERICAN WRITER

*T*he kitchen is the heart of the communal cause.

Marialisa Calta
20th-century American writer

I don't like to say that my kitchen is a religious place, but I would say that if I were a voodoo princess, I would conduct my rituals there.

Pearl Bailey (1918–1990)
American singer

I watched how Mother got satisfaction from cooking and making others happy. It took me a little while to understand this was a mission in *my* life too.

PAUL PRUDHOMME (B. 1940)
AMERICAN CHEF

. . . it's nice for two to work together on something they can

sit down afterward and eat.

Nancy Price (b. 1925)
American writer